Whose Is It? Science

Whose Mouth Is This?

A Look at Bills, Suckers, and Tubes

Written by Lisa Morris Kee
Illustrated by Ken Landmark

Content Advisor: Julie Dunlap, Ph.D.

Reading Advisor: Lauren A. Liang, M.A.

Literacy Education, University of Minnesota

Minneapolis, Minnesota

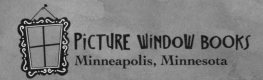

PICTURE WINDOW BOOKS
Minneapolis, Minnesota

To Elisabeth Kee, my groovy girl—L.M.K.

Editor: Nadia Higgins
Designer: Melissa Voda
Page production: The Design Lab
The illustrations in this book were prepared digitally.

Printed in the United States of America.

Library of Congress Cataloging-in-Publication Data
Kee, Lisa Morris, 1962–
  Whose mouth is this? : a look at bills, suckers, and tubes / written by Lisa Kee; illustrated by Ken Landmark.
     p. cm.
  Summary: Explores the variety of mouths found in the animal kingdom, including the puffin's bill, howler monkey's mouth, and butterfly's tube, and describes how they are used.
  ISBN 1-4048-0008-5 (lib. bdg)
  1. Mouth-Juvenile literature. [1. Mouth. 2. Animals-Food.] I. Landmark, Ken, ill. II. Title.
  QL857 .K44 2003
  573.3'5—dc21   2002007317

Picture Window Books
5115 Excelsior Boulevard
Suite 232
Minneapolis, MN 55416
1-877-845-8392
www.picturewindowbooks.com

Chew on this clue and see who's who.

Look closely at an animal's mouth. A mouth can be a long tube or a sticky suction cup. Mouths can be as tiny as pinheads or as big as garage doors.

Mouths tell you how an animal eats or how it holds on to things. One look at an animal's sharp fangs warns you to stay away.

Mouths don't all look alike, because they don't all work alike.

Can you tell whose mouth is whose?

Look in the back for more fun facts about mouths.

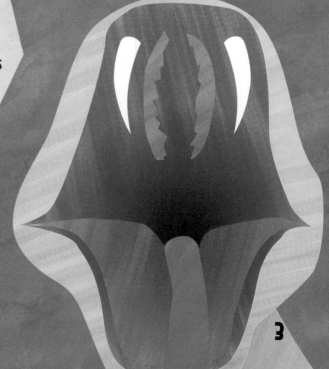

3

Whose mouth is this, howling in the forest?

4

This is a howler monkey's mouth.

As the sun rises in the rain forest, howler monkeys gather in groups. Together, they let out a great roar. The roar echoes through the trees and tells other howler monkeys, "Keep out!"

Fun fact: A howler monkey's wide mouth and throat work like a megaphone. Lots of other monkeys shriek, chatter, and scold each other, but the howler monkey's cry is the loudest. A howler monkey can be heard more than a mile away.

Whose mouth is this, curled up tight?

7

This is a butterfly's mouth.

A butterfly's mouth is a long tube that works like a straw. The butterfly stretches out its mouth to suck nectar from a flower. When the butterfly is done drinking, the tube curls back up under the butterfly's head.

Fun fact: Other insects have tube mouths, too. The mosquito uses its tube mouth to bite animals and people and suck up their blood.

8

Whose mouth is this, so strange and round?

This is a sea lamprey's mouth.

A sea lamprey is a fish that looks like a snake.
A sea lamprey's mouth is a powerful sucker.
The lamprey sticks its mouth onto the side of
a fish, then the lamprey digs in its sharp teeth
and eats the fish.

Fun fact: A female sea lamprey
uses her mouth to pick up and
move small rocks on the bottom
of a stream. She clears a place
and makes the perfect spot to
keep her eggs safe.

Whose mouth is this, so big and wide?

11

This is a blue whale's mouth.

This whale's mouth has baleen plates instead of teeth. Baleen works like a strainer. The whale takes in a huge mouthful of seawater. When the whale squirts the water back out, tiny sea creatures are trapped behind the baleen.

Fun fact: Blue whales are the largest animals on Earth, but they eat some of the smallest living things. Every time the whale fills its mouth, it traps thousands of tiny shellfish called krill.

Whose mouth is this, carrying a cub?

13

This is a leopard's mouth.

A mother leopard uses her powerful mouth to gently lift her cub and move it away from danger. A leopard also uses its sharp teeth and strong jaws to kill its prey.

Fun fact: A leopard uses its mouth to drag its food up into a tree. It hides the food where other hungry animals can't reach it.

Whose mouth is this, so full of fish?

15

This is a puffin's bill.

A puffin dives into the sea and scoops up fish in its rounded bill. The puffin can swallow fish underwater, or it can carry fish back to its nest. Bumps in the puffin's bill help it grip lots of fish as it swims or flies.

Fun fact: A puffin cleans its feathers by pulling them through its bill. This is called preening. As a puffin preens, it spreads a waxy oil on its feathers to make them waterproof.

Whose mouth is this, with glistening fangs?

This is a pit viper's mouth.

The pit viper opens its mouth to strike. Sharp fangs swing forward. When the snake bites, deadly poison flows through the fangs and into its prey.

Fun fact: The pit viper's jaws can stretch and open very wide. A pit viper can swallow an animal bigger than the snake's own head.

Whose mouth is this, eating an ice-cream cone?

This is your mouth!

Like other animals, you can eat, breathe, and taste with your mouth. You can drink water through a straw. You can howl like a monkey. Can you squirt water out of your mouth like a whale? You are the only animal that can tell jokes with your mouth. What else does your mouth do?

Fun fact: Did you know that it's more work to frown than to smile? We use over twice as many muscles to frown as we do to smile.

20

Just for Fun

Can you cross the crocodile swamp? Point to the rocks with the right answers and make your way to dry land.

A bird that catches fish in its bill is a

peacock   puffin   muffin

When a pit viper is ready to strike, its fangs fill with

blood   root beer   poison

A blue whale uses its baleen to strain

sharks   spaghetti and meatballs   tiny sea creatures

A howler monkey's cries tell other monkeys to

wake up!   keep out!   twist and shout!

A butterfly uses its long tube mouth to

bite   drink nectar   shoot watermelon seeds

Whew! You made it!

Fun Facts About Mouths

TRICK MOUTHS The alligator snapping turtle has a flap of skin in its mouth that looks just like a worm. The snapping turtle lies still under water with its mouth open wide. When a fish swims up to eat the fake worm, the snapping turtle snaps its jaws shut and eats the fish.

BUSY MOUTHS To build a home, a beaver cuts down trees with its teeth. The beaver carries a tree in its mouth as it walks and swims. Its strong front teeth never stop growing. Beavers chew almost all the time to keep their teeth sharp.

ON THE TIPS OF THEIR TONGUES A chameleon's long tongue is sticky at the end. The lizard shoots out its tongue to catch a bug flying by. Snakes have forked tongues. They flick out their tongues to pick up the smells around them.

SQUID BEAKS A squid is a sea creature with a long, soft body. The only hard part of the squid is its mouth, which looks like a parrot's beak. The squid's pointed jaws bite its food into small pieces.

FANGS A LOT Many creatures besides snakes have deadly fangs. A tarantula spider's fangs are sharp and hollow. The Gila monster, a kind of lizard, has a poisonous bite. Its venom flows out of grooves in its bottom teeth.

ITCHY SPIT It's not the mosquito's bite that makes us itch. It's the mosquito's spit, or saliva. A mosquito's saliva has a special ingredient that keeps blood flowing easily up the mosquito's mouth. That ingredient is what makes a mosquito's bite so itchy.

Words to Know

baleen Baleen plates hang down on each side of a blue whale's mouth. Blue whales use baleen like a strainer to trap tiny animals inside their mouths.

bill A bird's bill is the hard, bony part of its mouth.

fang A fang is like a long, sharp tooth. Some fangs are hollow so poisonous venom can flow through them.

jaws Jaws are the hard part of the mouth that can move up or down to open and close it.

preen A bird preens when it cleans its feathers with its bill.

prey Animals that are hunted and eaten by other animals are prey.

To Learn More

AT THE LIBRARY

Berger, Melvin and Gilda. *Do Tarantulas Have Teeth?: Questions and Answers About Poisonous Creatures.* New York: Scholastic Reference, 1999.

Moses, Brian. *Munching, Crunching, Sniffing and Snooping.* New York: DK Publishing, 1999.

Scott, Janine. *Animal Senses.* Minneapolis: Compass Point Books, 2002.

Swanson, Diane. *Animals Eat the Weirdest Things.* New York: Holt, 1998.

ON THE WEB

Lincoln Park Zoo

http://www.lpzoo.com

Explore the animals at the Lincoln Park Zoo.

San Diego Zoo

http://www.sandiegozoo.org

Learn about animals and their habitats.

Want to learn more about animal mouths?

Visit FACT HOUND at

http://www.facthound.com

Index